CW01501036

This book is dedicated to George. His encouragement and support enabled me to develop from a drab caterpillar into a flamboyant butterfly.

My thanks go to my husband Chris for his support and help whilst writing this book and to everyone who contributed the quotes scattered throughout it.

Dancing Through *the* Decades

Dancing Through *the* Decades

'60s '70s '80s '90s '00s '10s '20s

Yvonne Wright

Troubador Publishing Ltd
Unit E2 Airfield Business Park
Harrison Road, Market Harborough
Leicestershire LE16 7UL
Tel: 0116 279 2299
Email: books@troubador.co.uk
Web: www.troubador.co.uk

ISBN 978 1 8362 810 54

British Library Cataloguing in Publication Data.
A catalogue record for this book is available from the British Library.

Typeset in 11pt Minion Pro by Troubador Publishing Ltd, Leicester, UK

Contents

Prologue

In recent years I have seen, and read, many reports in the media about the winter of 1962–3. It is thought to be by some as the hardest Great Britain has had since 1740.

Public transport was several times brought to a standstill and the January power crisis was grave enough to provoke an emergency meeting of the Cabinet. It was a winter to remember. There are reports of cars being driven over frozen rivers. There was a power crisis so severe that it was discussed by the Cabinet. It was called by some The Big Freeze and it was a winter to remember for those who experienced it.

And remember it, I do. When it started snowing, just after Christmas, I was delighted and, for a couple of days, I built snowmen in the garden and threw the odd snowball at my dad, but by the end of the school holidays, the snow had frozen hard. It remained that way until the spring.

I was in the last year of junior school (Year 6) and looking forward to moving to big school in September. I lived close to school and usually walked it in about six minutes, but in January 1963, it took much longer. Clambering over frozen mini mountains of snow and slithering along pavements soon became a drag. It was always 'wet playtime' at school and snowballing was banned due to the dangers of ice. We would sit in class with our coats on if the school ran out of coal. If we ran out of coal at home, we would wrap ourselves in blankets. There were times when the power went off and we sat in darkness till bedtime, and I would try to read by the light of the coal fire when candles were unavailable.

Mum struggled to get to the shops for food and the vans selling bread and vegetables could not get down our street. My dad couldn't cycle to work so had to take the bus then walk to work, so, in effect, his shifts lasted longer.

We didn't moan – there was no point – but we did get fed up. When the temperatures rose and the ice gradually melted, we felt that we were being released from some sort of hibernation and could restart our lives. We wanted to get out and about. We wanted new opportunities. My new opportunity was amazing and I'm still enjoying it sixty years later.

Dancing has always been part of my life. From my earliest memory of country dancing lessons at my primary school to the most recent Christmas show with the Willingdon School of Dancing, dance has been a hugely important and defining aspect of who I am. Coming from a difficult family dynamic, and an unhappy childhood, dancing gave me the freedom to be me. Freedom to express myself when no-one was listening, freedom to move when I felt restricted by loneliness, and above all freedom to let go of sadness and regret.
Dancing is simply movement, either to music, or perhaps just in silence. I found a peace and an inner world that took me to beautiful far off places, where I could escape my troubled life. Dancing is the perfect way to create something that only you know how to interpret. To me it is quite simply joy.

Lucy, Eastbourne

First Steps

In March 1963, my friend Linda told me that a children's ballroom dancing class had started in town. She asked if I wanted to go with her that coming Saturday. Would I? You bet, but there was the problem of my mother. She was only 4 feet 10 inches tall and tiny, like a doll, but she was a force to be reckoned with, especially if dancing was involved.

My earliest memories are of skipping and dancing around our back garden to music I'd remembered from the radio. From the age of five, I'd begged my mother to let me go to ballet classes. The answer was always a resounding no.

"No! It's a waste of time and money."

The reason for this is that she herself had trained in ballet from a very young age until she was a teenager. She had often told me how, in the school shows, she burst out of gigantic cakes and tap danced on stage on pointe. However, she was forced to give it up in her teens by her father. She did not have the skills to train as a teacher, and to be a professional ballet dancer in the 1920s was considered to be tantamount to being a 'lady of the night'. This left her very bitter towards dance. I didn't think this was fair on me, but I was in the school country dancing team and made do with that. I wanted to attend the ballroom class with Linda more than anything.

On the way home from school, I prepared myself for another refusal but prayed that I would be allowed to go. I decided to wait until Dad was home from work and ask during tea because he was usually on my side and might be able to talk her round.

My prayers were answered. After tea, I was sent out of the room whilst my parents talked about my request.

A few minutes later, Mum called me back into the kitchen and said, "Well, ballroom dancing might be useful when you grow up, so you can go. I'll go and see Linda's mum in the morning and sort out the arrangements."

My dad winked at me, and I jumped up and down with excitement, saying, "Thank you, thank you, thank you."

I knew a little about ballroom dancing, as my mum and dad sometimes used to take me to a social club on a Saturday night, where I saw men and women, including my parents, dancing around the floor and occasionally I would stand on my dad's size eleven feet and dance round with him. I wanted to learn this skill and spent the rest of the week looking forward to my first class.

On Saturday morning, Mum and I set off down the road and met Linda and her mum on the junction with their road. I strode off proudly wearing my Sunday best clothes. We all got on the bus to town and when it stopped, right outside one of the cinemas, Mum told us all to get off. She pointed to the right-hand side of the cinema where there was a set of double doors. One of the doors was open and we could see other children going through it. The four of us followed them and started to climb three flights of stairs to the ballroom. I was to find out many years later that this used to be a café for the cinema.

We found ourselves in a queue and then slowly climbed to another door. There was a beautiful lady looking glamourous at a desk by the entrance. She had a lovely smile and asked Linda and I to wait to one side whilst she took our details from our mums.

As I walked forward, I gazed in amazement at the huge windows, red velvet seats and a large geometric light fitting attached to the ceiling. There were lots of children sitting down, some eating sweets and drinking pop, which they had bought from a café area. There was music playing. It came from a big desk on the far side of the room. What impressed me most, however, was the floor. I had seen dance floors before when my parents had taken me to social clubs and those on the end of many piers, but this floor shone and gleamed. It looked too beautiful to walk on and I did notice that children were walking around rather than over it.

Our mums left. The music stopped and then a man appeared, together with the glamourous lady. They beckoned us onto the floor and started the class. All the new starters were asked to stand at one side of the floor and wait. The music restarted and the other children began to dance round the room. The glamourous lady, whose name I have forgotten, then led the rest of us through another door which led into a cloakroom with coat racks around the outside, just like the ones at school. However, there was an area in the middle which was our dance floor. The lady told us she would teach us the Quickstep.

I had no idea what a Quickstep was, but I listened and watched very carefully as she demonstrated the steps. It looked quite easy, but my feet didn't seem to go where they were supposed to go. However, the teacher told us we had all done well and would get better with practice.

We all then returned to the ballroom and watched the more experienced children dancing to the music. None of them had a partner but they all stood up tall and held their arms up as if they did have one. The man then announced it was fun time. He put on a twist record, and we all joined in, dancing until we had stitch. Then he got us to form a big circle. Linda and I copied the others doing a dance called the Hokey Cokey. I wish I had a pound for every time I've danced that since.

Finally, it was time to go. Our mums were waiting at the bottom of the stairs, along with many others, and we caught the bus home.

When we got home, I told my mum about the class, and how much I'd enjoyed it.

I thanked her for taking me, but then she said, "I'm glad you enjoyed it but don't expect to be good at it because of your ankles; they are very weak. Remember, the doctors said you would never walk when you were born so don't expect too much."

My ankles and feet had always been a problem. I mentioned that my mum was very small and petite; my dad could circle her waist with his hands easily. Well, I wasn't born until my mum was in her late thirties; her first and only pregnancy. I was a healthy baby that weighed in at 8lbs 8ozs – 3.85kg in metric. I was so big that I had filled her womb completely. My legs had never been able to unfold, and I was born with my feet joined to my bottom. The birth, which happened during a massive power cut, must have torn my mother's insides apart. Indeed, she needed a hysterectomy and developed rheumatic fever, which left her with a serious heart condition. Surgeons operated on me shortly after my birth to try and straighten my legs. My knees didn't straighten completely so I was put into splints, my feet dangling down in pointe position. My mum was given instructions on how to massage my feet and ankles daily. Thanks to her, I did learn to walk but I could only do so on my tiptoes. I wore shoes with built up heels and, in fact, I was in my forties before I could walk on a flat foot.

However, I wasn't going to let any of that hold me back. I told my mum that as I had learnt to walk, then I would learn to dance properly.

From then on, Linda and I attended every Saturday, and I started to gain a little independence as Mum would give me my class fee plus sixpence to buy a snack when she dropped us off at the door. I gained confidence and made new friends as I learnt Rock and Roll, Cha Cha Cha, and several party dances. We danced the twist every week and I became so good that I entered a competition held on the end of the pier when we went on holiday. I didn't win but I made it to the final and that did wonders for my self-esteem.

DID YOU KNOW?

Chubby Checker released a record called 'The Twist' in 1960 and it went to number one in the charts. In 1962, it was released again and went to number one again.

However, every week, we were sent into the cloakroom to improve and practise our Quickstep. After a few months, we started to get bored, and we wanted to learn more dances. Towards the end of the summer term, my friend Linda said...

– What she said next got me excited again and set me off on my fabulous journey.

CHAPTER 2

Moving On

Linda told me of another dancing school that had started a children's class, so we decided we would go there next Saturday. When we got off the bus, in the marketplace, Mum led us to an impressive building opposite the museum. The ground floor had been converted into shops, but Mum stopped outside a large doorway. There was an enormous, ornate, metal door handle. Mum opened the door, and we went through. We found ourselves in a space which was mostly taken up by a beautiful staircase. The spindles, supporting the banister rail, were made from wrought iron and the rail itself was highly polished, dark-brown wood, which curled around at the bottom.

I could hear it calling to me: "Slide down me."

The staircase itself was so wide that the three of us were able to walk up side by side with plenty of room to spare. We climbed two flights of stairs and reached a large landing. There were several doors but none of them indicated a dancing school, so we climbed another two flights. We reached an identical landing but this time there were several children and their mums waiting there.

Just as we reached the top step, a door opened, and another glamourous lady walked out onto the landing. She had blonde hair piled high on her head, was carrying a white poodle dog under her arm, and was wearing a pair of high-heeled gold shoes. I was impressed.

"Hello, everyone," she said. "My name is Jean. Welcome to our dance school. Please form a queue."

After a short wait, we walked through the door and entered a small vestibule. There was an office to the right, where Jean was taking the class fees, a small cloakroom to the left, and in front of me was another shiny, glossy dance floor. The room was lined on two sides with high-backed chairs and small round tables. In front of me to the left were the record decks and shelves holding the records, whilst to the right were a few blue comfy chairs.

Jean told us a few rules, which included, "Do not slide down the bannisters."

I did once break this rule when someone dared me to do so, but, as I nearly fell off, I never repeated it. Jean told us that we were going to learn the Waltz, so I was excited to be learning a new dance. Once we had learnt how to dance a box step, I was partnered up with one of the boys in the group; I think there were two. We were taught how to hold each other then we had to work out how our feet worked together. We seemed to manage this okay, but the boy never appeared after that first week. I do hope that wasn't my fault.

I attended regularly and gradually increased both my knowledge and skill, but for years I kept forgetting which foot to start with. After some time, we were told that, if we wished, we could stay for the general dancing time. This had two benefits to me. Firstly, the time I spent in the dancing school was two hours, and this was too long for my mum to hang around in town. So, I started travelling there and back independently. Secondly, there was a short break between the two sessions. We were permitted to go down to the floor below where we could buy a bottle of pop and a packet of crisps. From then on, every Saturday morning, my mum would count out enough money for my bus fares, class fees and refreshments. When any of these rose in price, the amount she gave me rose accordingly. This was my first lesson in money management as, if I wanted to save up for something, I could forego the refreshments and save up the cash.

My class focussed on three dances: the Waltz, the Quickstep, and the Slow Foxtrot. The Foxtrot was hard to learn as all the girls had to master the 'heel turn'. It is a beautiful, graceful dance but I'm not sure we did it justice in the early days. One day, the teacher told us we would be taking our bronze medal examination in a few weeks. This was both exciting and scary – an exam!

The exam was on a Sunday afternoon. I arrived early; I have a fear of being late and, to this day, I arrive early for everything. I wore my best dress. It was a white dress with a scalloped collar and a very full skirt. It had been made for my recent confirmation and I thought it was beautiful. However, I was absolutely terrified and have no memory of dancing the exam.

We were told we had to wear dance shoes with a heel no higher than 1 inch (2.5cm). My grandmother had already bought me dancing shoes but, due to my walking problem and extremely high instep, they had 2-inch heels. It is no wonder then that, as I was wearing the regulation shoes, the examiner wrote on my report, 'some heel leads missed'.

This brought my marks down and reminded me of my mother telling me, "Don't expect to be good at it (dancing)."

I did not let this get me down too much. I never showed her the report and once I was old enough to wear higher heels, making a good heel lead became much easier.

When we arrived for class the following Saturday, there was a list of our names pinned up on a notice board giving the results. I was too scared to look so someone else gave me the good news that I had passed.

A few weeks later, those who had passed their exam were presented with a bronze medal that had the initials IDMA. This stood for the International Dance Masters Association. A few years later, it amalgamated with another dance organisation, the Dance Teachers Association, and became the IDTA: International Dance Teachers Association. I am so proud to now be a life member of this organisation.

On the back of the medal, I found my name had been engraved together with the date of the examination. In addition to the medal, we were presented with a certificate and a small bronze badge, which I was proud to wear on the lapel of my school blazer.

Over the years, I progressed through the medal system in both ballroom (Waltz, Quickstep, Foxtrot and Tango) and Latin American (Cha Cha Cha, Rumba, Samba and Jive). I didn't learn the Paso Doble and Viennese Waltz until I was much older.

As my dancing progressed, my class got later in the day. So, I helped the beginners, joined in the practice session, and then spent time in the museum or shopping in town while I waited for my class. I loved every minute.

Now, please don't get the idea that I was a square ('uncool' in today's language). I was anything but. I loved pop music and watched *Top of the Pops* from its first broadcast. By watching that programme, I learnt how to dance to the music in the charts and what the London fashions were. I had very little money to buy clothes but by getting a weekend job in a newsagent's shop, I could afford to buy material from the market and make my own trendy clothes. I was also part of a young persons' committee at my local church. We raised money to train guide dogs for the blind in two ways;we did an annual sponsored walk of twenty-six miles and ran a disco in the church hall on alternate Wednesdays. All the members of the committee brought along their latest records, which we played for the young people of the area. It was great fun, and I learnt skills invaluable to me when I started my own dancing school. Disco started well before *Saturday Night Fever*.

I recently came across a book by Doris Lavelle called *Discotheque Dancing*. She self-published this in 1970 and it contains descriptions, and photos, of movements we were dancing at that time.

As teenagers, my friends and I enjoyed dancing at discos to the records released by our favourite groups, not bands. Bands referred to the big bands our parents listened to. I especially liked The Kinks, The Animals and The Rolling Stones. We would stand in a circle moving to the music, but one person would move to the centre and dance their signature moves. When they moved back to their place, someone else would replace them. This style of dancing meant boys were not holding the girls, but that no longer mattered. In our parents' time, dancing with someone was often the only time you could have physical contact with someone to whom you were attracted. Our generation, however, were in the 'permissive society' and the previous rule book was thrown out of the window. We would kiss and cuddle in public, but we often heard members of the older generation tut tutting and making comments about the 'younger generation'.

It was particularly important to me to get good O-level results, as I wanted to go to either university or college in order to escape difficulties at home. This self-imposed pressure caused me great stress and my dancing acted as the release button of the pressure cooker of my mental health.

O-levels changed to A-levels. Children's classes moved onto private lessons, and I started going to lots of adult classes with a boy from the dancing school.

When I started in the upper sixth (Year 13), my partner and I decided that we had learnt a lot about ballroom dancing but would like to learn Old Time, now known as Classical Sequence. We had seen it on *Come Dancing*, the predecessor of *Strictly*. My friend Janet, not Linda this time, who was in year below me at school, had been doing this style of dance since she was young. She introduced us to her teacher, and we arranged to start private lessons with him.

DID YOU KNOW?
Henry Fox created the Foxtrot in 1914.

Dancing has meant a new lease of life, after being widowed and moving home. It has afforded me a new circle of friends.

Viv, Eastbourne

CHAPTER 3

A Glamourous World

For our sequence lessons, we went to the Railway Institute. As my father worked for the railway, I had been here many times before for children's Christmas parties and the like. However, I had never been in the ballroom. To reach it, we ascended a magnificent staircase and entered through double doors. The room was decorated in blue and gold. It was larger than either of my other dancing schools and had ornate pillars to support the roof. I was impressed.

Our first lesson with Harry, the new teacher, was a revelation. At the start, he told us that his was a competitive school, and we could only receive tuition if we agreed to being trained as competitors. I thought this was a wonderful opportunity and felt tremendously excited about this idea, my partner less so, but we both agreed to Harry's terms. His wife Dorothy then explained that I needed to wear a full circle skirt, with underskirts, for all my lessons, but as I was an adult, I did not have to wear one of the blue uniform dresses that the younger girls wore.

Harry taught us the Veleta and told us that we needed to learn how to use our arms when dancing Old Time (Classical Sequence), so I arrived for my next lesson wearing my circular rock and roll skirt with two 'paper' underskirts beneath it. Paper underskirts were made of a stiff material. They had several layers, often multicoloured, which were worn by girls in the 1950s. When the girls danced spins, their skirts and underskirts would spin out too.

In that second lesson, we were taught the Boston Two Step. We had danced this previously at social dances, but this version was vastly different, as we had to dance it technically correctly. This meant we had to learn a step called the pas de basque. People often struggle with that step, but our experience of the Samba bounce action made it a little easier for us.

Harry told us we would be taking both our bronze and silver medals at his next medal examination session. The exam rules had eased a little by then. Only two dances were needed for a bronze medal and three for a silver medal; previously this had been three and four respectively. He also explained that for our silver medal, one of the dances had to be the Old-Time Waltz. The other two would be the Saunter Reve and the Tango Serida. All sequence dances have their own name because everyone is meant to be dancing the same steps in a set routine in a circle around the room, so the name of the dance is always announced before the dance starts. One of the reasons people enjoy sequence dancing is that you are less likely to be bumped into, or bump into, other dancers. However, nowadays, people are less likely to dance Old Time (known as Classical today) due to the technical skill needed and much more likely to dance Modern Sequence, i.e. based on today's ballroom and Latin dances.

I dedicated myself to learning, and perfecting, the steps, but what I enjoyed the most, and still do, was the lifting, lowering, folding, and unfolding of the arms. Classical sequence, is, for me, the most graceful of the ballroom dance genres. It also involves turning the head at key moments in each dance. It is based on the five foot positions of ballet. My favourite dance is the Fylde Waltz and if I find myself in an empty ballroom, I will often dance it solo. Executing the correct footwork and making the precise foot positions gives me a sense of worth and it is good for my breathing in a comparable way to yoga.

I was told I needed to wear a full circle skirted dress for my medal exams. I could not afford a new dress. However, I had already made a ¾ circle skirted dress for my last ballroom exam. It was made from lightweight brocade and had a tiny pink and silver check design, so I bought one yard (almost one metre) of silver lamé. I cut two triangular pieces and inserted them as godets into the skirt of my pink and silver dress. I was also able to borrow a lovely white net underskirt to wear beneath it. I felt like the ballerina I had dreamt of being since childhood and I danced better in those exams than I had ever danced before. This was because I felt special and like a real dancer. I received excellent marks and finally put my mum's 'don't expect to be any good' comment into a mental dustbin forever.

After the exams, Harry started to prepare us for the competitive world. He told us that we had a few months to prepare for the Filey Dance Festival, which had a whole week of competitions. However, this fell when I was taking my A-levels; fortunately, it did not clash with any of my exams. In the meantime, we took part in some local competitions and took our gold medal before going to Filey the following year. For competitions, I needed a proper competition gown. Dorothy showed me the pattern I needed and told me of a company that sold everything I needed. There was no online shopping in those days, so my partner drove me to the next town, where the company was based, to buy the materials.

I had learnt dressmaking at school and had an electric sewing machine but making that first gown really taught me how to sew. The dresses you see on *Strictly* are much lighter, floatier, and easier to wear than my dress. The bodice required lining, interfacing, chiffon, and boning. The skirt needed yards of net which had to be cut, gathered, and assembled into a huge underskirt then topped by two layers of chiffon. Once the basic dress had been assembled, it needed to be decorated. My first gown was bright blue trimmed with yards of daisy flower lace to which I glued hundreds of blue and white rhinestones. As you can imagine, this took me some time and lots of patience.

My partner also had to acquire his outfit. He was required to wear a formal white starched shirt with a wing collar, a white bow tie, a white waistcoat, white braces, a black tail suit and white gloves. The shirt was fastened with a set of studs. We had a few gentlemen's outfitters in town where all these articles could be bought but the cost of a tail suit was out of our budget. We were lucky enough to find such a suit in the small ads of our local paper, which we could afford. However, it was several sizes too big. My partner's mother was an excellent dressmaker, although she had no training in tailoring. Nevertheless, she took the suit apart, resized each piece and remade it. This was a major undertaking; the end result was as good as anything that could be bought in the shops. She did an amazing job.

I had very long hair, so I went to my hairdresser, Brenda, to have my hair put up for competitions. She would wash my hair and put it in rollers before putting me under the dryer for what seemed like ages. Once dry, my hair would be backcombed before being rolled, curled, and pinned on top of my head. Then she would glue it in place with hairspray. If I had a competition on a Sunday, I would keep my hair up until Monday evening, as I had to unpin it and wash it thoroughly to get all the backcombing and hairspray out.

Once I was clad in my gown, with my hair up, wearing matching jewellery and in full make up, all my everyday worries and concerns disappeared. I came alive and just wanted to step onto the floor and perform.

During my last year of teacher training college, I had to forgo competitions due to the demands of my course and the expense of getting married to my partner once I had qualified, so I made sure I attended as many social dances as possible to fill my desire to dance.

Dance has given me confidence I didn't know I had. Before dancing, I would never have believed I'd be performing on a stage.

Sam, Eastbourne

CHAPTER 4

Continuing with Competitions

Once married, we decided to return to our ballroom roots, and by Christmas, I was entering ballroom and Latin competitions. We had returned to the ballroom I had first attended but it was now under new management. Our new coach, George, was a hard taskmaster, but I learnt such a lot from him, for which I am eternally grateful. He had been trained in Latin American by Monsieur Pierre and in ballroom by Charles Frost, and, for him, technique was extremely important. Until having lessons with George, I hated dancing the Slow Foxtrot. This was due to the fact that my heel turns never felt quite right. When I told him that this was the reason we wanted to concentrate on Latin rather than ballroom competitions, he took me to the centre of the floor and within ten minutes I had learnt how to dance the perfect heel turn. From that moment, I came to love the Foxtrot, and it has been my favourite ballroom dance for decades. My struggle to learn how to dance a heel turn, together with George's excellent teaching of it, has enabled me to help all my pupils learn this key step in the Foxtrot.

Although I had qualified as a schoolteacher in the summer, I was not able to get a teaching post until the following January, so, in order to help pay the mortgage and other bills, I got a job as a shop assistant in British Home Stores. The store was only a few hundred yards from the dancing school; fortunate, as our weekly lesson was at 6.15pm and I did not finish work until 6pm. I just had enough time to get to the studio and change my shoes before going onto the dance floor.

George, like all teachers, had his personal teaching methods. The first was used to ensure we maintained body contact during our ballroom dances. George would tell us to take the ballroom hold, make any minor changes to improve it and then place an LP (album) record sleeve in between our two bodies. He would then play music, and we would dance. To begin with, it was not long before the sleeve went flying. When we moaned about this exercise, we were told that we should be grateful because when he was being trained, he and his partner had to dance keeping a flat iron between them, which was very painful if you let it slip. Although there were no uniform rules, like those imposed by Harry, George made my partner wear a jacket to dance ballroom; in order to improve his posture, George would sometimes make him put a wooden coat hanger, minus the hook, inside his jacket and then dance. One of my faults when we started going to George was that I turned my head too far to right when going to promenade position in the Tango. He told me I was in danger of getting 'Blackpool neck' and needed to reduce the amount of turn I made with my head. He told me to look straight forward and imagine the divisions of a clock face. I had to practise turning my head between eleven o'clock and one o'clock only. He would then play a Tango. My partner and I would dance whilst George stayed behind me with his hands either side of my face about three centimetres away; if I turned my head too far, I would effectively slap my own face onto his hands. I quickly rectified the fault. We made good progress, but in addition to our lessons, we needed a lot of practice. On Monday nights, we went to the Locarno and danced to the Ray McVay band; on Wednesday, we went to a dance at my partner's works ballroom; on Thursday, we attended an advanced practice night at the dancing school; and on Fridays, we, together with a few other competitive couples at the school, hired a school hall and organised our own music. This left the weekends clear for competitions.

One of my proudest achievements during this period was being picked to dance in a team match between our town and its future twin town in Germany. We took some of the top juveniles (under 12s) with us, as, at that time, there were no competitions for that age group in Germany. Some of them went on to be adult champions. The following year, the German team came to us for a rematch as part of the twinning celebrations.

Unfortunately, after a few years coaching us, George was taken seriously ill. I received a phone call. George's wife Vera told me that our lessons were cancelled until further notice, as George was ill, but she did not specify what was the matter with him. A couple of weeks later, we were told he had been diagnosed with a serious heart condition and George had asked to see us both. We had no idea what he wanted to talk to us about. We arranged a date and time. This meeting led to me taking another new turning along my dancing journey.

Living with chronic pain and fatigue would not make me think of dancing. But I have danced since I was a young child and losing the ability to enjoy dance when I was ill was hard when I fell ill. As I improved and was able to move gently, basic dancing exercises rebuilt my strength and stamina. It also gave me joy because it was not rigid exercises, it was reminding my brain of the joy of movement. Even if I am down, dance provides escape, whether it is a few exercises, a routine or a full show. Over the years, dancing has given me freedom to express myself, enjoy and experience life regardless of my illness.

Helen, Eastbourne

CHAPTER 5

From Amateur to Professional

George was seated at a table when we arrived, and he beckoned us to sit down too. I do not remember much about that meeting, or the days which followed it, as what he said was so unexpected.

He told us he needed a young couple to train as teachers to take some of the strain from him. He wanted us to be those teachers. I was a teacher in a local primary school, but I had never thought about becoming a teacher of dancing, nor of teaching adults.

He explained the terms and conditions. If we accepted, we would attend classes four nights a week and assist with the teaching. In addition, we would be needed to attend the Saturday night dance to help out by partnering people and playing music for them to dance to. I was also needed on Saturday mornings to assist with teaching the junior classes. In return, we would attend the studio on Sunday mornings for two hours in order to learn the theory of ballroom dancing.

It was a lot to take in and we needed time to think about his proposal, as it was such a big decision. We considered the pros and cons...

Con: If we accepted, then there would be no more entering competitions, which I loved.

Pros: Being a competitor was becoming increasingly expensive and we did not have time for anything else. Also, my husband and my parents wanted me to have a baby.

The pros won. We saw George again and told him we would accept his offer. He was delighted. He told me to arrive at 9am on Saturday morning to help with juniors and that our first theory lesson would be the following day at 10am. I had not expected things to happen quite so quickly.

The following days were quite overwhelming. On Saturday morning, I mounted the three flights of steps up to the studio with trepidation and opened the door apprehensively.

I had only just said, "Hello," to Vera when a young girl ran up to me and said, "Hello, Miss. My name is Diane. Are you going to be my new teacher?"

Before I could answer, George appeared and said, "Yes, Yvonne will be helping from now on."

The children's classes were much as I remembered mine to be. I seem to remember there were three classes: beginners, intermediate and advanced. I was to assist with Diane's class, the intermediates.

I am still a friend of Diane. She went on to qualify as a dance teacher with the IDTA herself and when we meet at conferences, we will partner each other. It is a standing joke that I will still advise her on posture and hold.

At the end of the morning, I had to help with clearing up and preparing the room for the Saturday night dance.

George came over and said to me, "I'm going to teach an important lesson about being a dance teacher now. Wait there."

I was wondering what on earth this new learning was when George reappeared with a very wide sweeping brush.

He said, "I'm going to teach you how to sweep a ballroom floor."

Then he did just that. There is a method to it and a clear floor is essential, as the tiniest bit of litter on a ballroom floor can cause you to slip. I have never forgotten that first mini lesson and always think of him when I sweep the floor before classes.

The next morning, my husband and I went to the studio. It was eerily quiet. George was waiting for us and gave us each a new blue textbook, A5 size. It was a technique book for ballroom dancing written by Alex Moore, a well-known man in the ballroom-dancing world. George told us, however, that within weeks there would be a new textbook written by Guy Howard which would supersede Alex's book. George used the blue book to show us which figures we needed to learn for our exam and outlined everything else we had to learn. The exam was be divided into two sections. We were required to give a short dance demonstration to start with, then the examiner would ask us questions and ask us to dance selected dance figures step by step, giving technical information about the steps at the same time. No-one would be allowed in the room with me during the exam apart from the examiner for this important section. I was a little disgruntled to find out that I had to do the dance demonstration twice, once as lady and then as gent, whereas my husband only had to dance as gent. I am pleased to say this is no longer the case.

We were there for two hours and when we left, my mind was buzzing with all the information we had been given and what George had asked us to study before the following Sunday. I had not realised how much there was to learn. Before we left, George showed us a small walk-in cupboard with a 'Staff Only' label on the door. It had coat hooks and small compartments to put dance shoes in. I put my dance shoes in an empty section. So that was it: I was a student teacher. I was 'staff'.

We returned the following day as requested to assist with the beginners' class, which ran from 8.15pm to 10.30pm. This was a real eye opener to me, as I had never been a social dancer. I had learnt one or two dances at a time. We had to be technically correct, e.g., correct footwork and timing, before taking an exam then moving on to new dances and additional figures. However, in an adult beginners' class, the pupils learnt a little bit of lots of dances. This included the Social, or Rhythm; Foxtrot, as it is sometimes called.

I only knew how to dance this because, at our previous exam session, as well as dancing for our higher-level ballroom and Latin medals, George had told us we had to take our POP test along with everyone else taking and exam. This was a new assessment created by the IDTA called the Popular Dance Test. This was aimed at social dancers who only had to dance the basic step of the Waltz, the Quickstep, and the Social Foxtrot. It later evolved into the Social Dance Award, which my pupils went on to take.

George refused to show us the Social Foxtrot and sent us to one of his beginners' classes, who were preparing for the exam, instead so we could follow them. There are only eight steps in the basic movement, and it is usually the first dance I teach to my adult beginners because they pick it up quickly and thereby gain confidence. The award for passing your POP test was a small pin badge. I was immensely proud of mine and still have it.

Another significant difference with the adult classes was the bar. George had been given a licence to serve alcohol so pupils would buy a drink on their way in, and most would buy another one in the interval. I was expected to serve behind the bar. Pouring pints and mixing snowballs became routine.

At the end of the evening, there was a strict regime for preparing for the next day. Cigarette ends were properly extinguished and collected into a metal box which was closed up in order to eliminate the risk of fire. Tables were cleared of rubbish and wiped. Chairs and tables were straightened, and all glasses were washed, dried, and put away. There were other people who helped with all these jobs, and it did not take long when we all worked as a team.

By the time we got home and to bed, it was usually about 11.30pm and I was up the next morning at 6am as I had to catch two buses to get to my school. I arrived at school at about 8.15am, taught all day and caught two more buses home. Then I had only a short time to eat, get ready and travel to the studio in the evening. My husband worked shifts, so I left a little earlier when he was on nights to catch the last bus, unless one of the pupils lived near me and offered me a lift. I did not drive, and we could not have afforded two cars anyway. When my husband was on 'afternoons', 2pm–10pm, I would travel straight to the studio from work and eat a sandwich before class. It was a rush, and I had to fit in lesson planning, marking and housework into the little free time I had, but I was still dancing, albeit at a less frantic pace, and I was learning all the time.

Things continued to move quickly. I became a student teacher in 1975. In 1976, I became pregnant and resigned my teaching post, giving birth to my elder daughter in 1977. That October, I passed my ballroom associate exam with the IDTA and became a qualified dance teacher. Unlike amateur medal exams, when you get your results fairly quickly, it is several weeks before you receive your professional results, and they come through the post. I was on tenterhooks for all that time, and anxiously watched for the postman every morning. It was such a relief to open my letter and find out I had passed. I was so pleased with myself.

I learnt a lot during my training. As well as dance theory and how to sweep the floor. I learnt:

- How to step onto a ballroom floor in front of a class, which could have 80+ people, and teach them.
- How to go up onto the music rostrum, play music and encourage people to get up and dance.

- When it was necessary, to add a one or two pence piece to the arm of the record player, so the needle did not slip.
- How to sit down with strangers and talk to them.

I moved from being chronically shy and withdrawn to being just quiet and shy. It was as if George knew what I was capable of and gently, but firmly, over time, drew me out of my thick shell.

After passing my exam, new dancing doors opened for me. I attended my first IDTA meeting in February 1978 at the Royal Lancaster Hotel, London. This visit was all arranged and paid for by George as a reward for passing the exam.

There were lectures during the day and George introduced me to so many dance professionals that it was a bit overwhelming. After the lectures, we all returned to our hotel to get ready for the dinner dance. Two couples from the dancing school, friends of George, had travelled down to London for the dinner dance. As there was eight of us, George ordered two taxis. The four ladies went in the first taxi and the men followed behind. When we arrived at the Lancaster, two doormen, dressed in tailcoats and top hats, opened the door for us and assisted us out of the taxi. I felt really important.

It was a very high-class event. A friend had loaned me a Frank Usher evening gown to wear. It was pale pink chiffon, and the bodice was covered with intricate beadwork. I felt like a princess in a strange land as I drifted in through the doors and found my seat. I remember seeing the menu and asking what 'sorbet' was. I remember everyone standing up for the president's arrival and clapping him in. I also remember being on the dance floor surrounded by current and ex-world class champions, many of them my dancing heroes. They, like myself, were not dancing fancy steps. They were dancing the Social Foxtrot and chatting to friends as they danced around the floor.

The evening ended eventually, and we all returned to our hotel, but I was unable to sleep. I kept reliving the sights and sounds of the evening because I wanted to remember everything. I was twenty-seven years old and now I felt like a grown up.

My thoughts on the benefits of dancing –
Good aerobic exercise.
Assisting mental agility by actually remembering the basic
steps and routines.
Body co-ordination, using feet and arms at the same time.
Stretching muscles not used daily.
Feel-good factor when dancing.
Improved confidence when dancing with others.
Having fun and enjoying new experiences.
Making new friends.

Ann, Eastbourne

CHAPTER 6

The Special Times

I worked for George for about fifteen years, and during that time I had some amazing experiences. I was privileged to watch many world champions give demonstrations. We had Len Goodman one Christmas and the men on the staff had to take down some of the Christmas decorations because when he lifted his partner above his head, she may have got tangled in them. Alan and Hazel Fletcher were one of my dance hero couples and they came to give a demonstration at the studio. This happened to be on my birthday. I got really excited when George told me that I could have a birthday dance with Alan, and even though we only danced the Social Foxtrot, dancing with him is one of my special dance memories. He gave me a signed photo of himself and his wife, which I kept. About ten years ago, I was seriously considering giving up teaching dancing when I went looking for something on a shelf. Suddenly, that photo fluttered down, landing at my feet, and at that moment, I decided to carry on.

On another occasion, we had a demonstration by Bill and Bobbie Irvine. Afterwards, Bill gave a lesson on moves we could do to disco music. We all smiled as we joined in with movements like 'answer the phone' and 'shake the maracas.'

The staff occasionally put on shows for the pupils. I remember once being put in front of a group singing "Bowl a bowl a bowl a penny a pitch." I was in front because of my enthusiastic movements but my microphone was not connected because I cannot sing.

A few months before I qualified, a new dance organisation was established called the Guild of Professional Teachers of Dancing. George joined and I signed up as a student member. We went to the first AGM, which was held during the World Championships at Blackpool. I had never been to this event before and found the atmosphere most exciting. I went into the Winter Gardens' main ballroom where the competitors were practising. There was ballroom music being played at one end and Latin music at the other; it was exhilarating. My daughter has the accolade of being the youngest person present at the guild meeting as she was about two months old.

George sometimes organised novelty nights when people had to dress up. One was a World War II night. I was about eight months pregnant, so I went as a GI bride, but I had an ordinary maternity dress with me in case I went into labour early. On another occasion, he arranged a 'tramp's supper'. I was almost nine months pregnant that time, so I put a set of 'normal' clothes in a bundle and fastened it to my tramp's stick. I told all the staff that if I went into labour, I was not going to hospital in a tramp's outfit. (I actually went past my due date on both occasions so danced a fast Jive every night from my due date until I went into labour.)

I taught all age groups, but my main focus was always the children. I ran a baby ballroom class for three- to five-year-olds when my girls were small. I had an interest in children with special and additional needs and this became my specialism when I returned to teaching in school. It was extremely rewarding to see children with a physical or learning difficulty overcome their barriers and learn to dance and see how it increased their confidence. However, I really came into my own once a certain film starring John Travolta hit the big screen.

Ballroom dancing is good for the soul, and uplifting. It is a worthwhile hobby to pursue, and it also keeps people fit. When footwork gets a little tricky, and the dancers get their feet mixed up, there are plenty of laughs in trying to try to get it right... I would recommend ballroom dancing to anyone, because as well as learning a new set of skills, and having a nice hobby to look forward to, it is a very good social outlet, and dancers can make some nice friends.
Tony, Eastbourne

Dance has benefited me by an improvement in fitness, and the opportunity to meet and chat with new people with a common interest. This keeps away the evil of depression.
Gil, Bournemouth

CHAPTER 7

Saturday Night Fever

By the mid '70s, many ballroom schools were finding it harder to recruit new pupils, particularly young adults. Ballroom dancing was seen as something older people did and it was no longer the means of meeting a new boyfriend or girlfriend. Then along came *Saturday Night Fever* in late 1977. The film was an enormous success and raised over $32 million. Not only did it breathe new life into dancing schools, but also new lighting and sound systems were developed for use in clubs. The clubs gave young people new, exciting venues where they could go and practise their new steps and movements.

I am sure many theses have been written on why this film transformed social dancing in this country, but here is my own opinion. When the young people watched this film, they saw lots of other young people, who looked and dressed like them, dancing in lines. Line Dancing has always been popular. I remember as a child learning the Madison, the Slosh, the Locomotion, and the March of the Mods, and, in later years, the Macarena and Oops Upside Your Head. Most of these dances were linked to a particular song in the charts, e.g., 'The Loco-Motion', so the dance disappeared when the song was no longer played. However, they were popular. Why? The answer is that the steps were simple and easy to pick up. Secondly, if you were not confident, you could get into the centre of the crowd where any mistakes would be less obvious; and thirdly, the desire to move to music and rhythm is within us all and always has been.

In addition to watching the dancing, cinema audiences were listening to brilliant, toe-tapping tunes. E.g., 'Stayin' Alive', which is now used by some people performing CPR to try and save someone's life.

There were many different dance scenes and although some people were able to mimic the iconic moves of John Travolta, the vast majority needed a little help to learn the steps and movements.

What the audiences did not realise at the time was that some of the dance scenes in the film were 'cut and paste'. The choreographer did teach several different dance routines which were filmed, but they appeared differently in the film. This made it harder for people to pick up routines just by watching. Therefore, the IDTA, and other dance organisations in the UK, set up lectures based on the original dance scripts to teach to their members. Those teachers then set up special classes to teach *Saturday Night Fever* dances. Our school had no sooner advertised our first class than we had to open a second one. Both classes were full for months. We also started to include it in our junior classes and quickly introduced it as a separate class.

It was not long before *Saturday Night Fever* dancing evolved into disco dancing. People were creating new disco routines all the time. I remember teaching 'The New York Bus Stop' to class after class of children. Another popular dance, with adults and children, was the Soul Cha Cha Cha. Only last year, I attended a dance fitness class where the Soul CCC was included and people today will still, on occasions such as weddings, get up and dance to 'Stayin' Alive'.

When I entered my first cache of pupils to take the new disco medals, George entered them under my name. As there was no professional disco qualification at that time, I received a special certificate from the IDTA stating that I had successfully entered pupils for disco examinations.

From then on, disco evolved into a dance genre in its own right. Some of my junior pupils, Diane amongst them, asked if they could form a disco formation team. Of course, I said yes, and soon we were entering pupils for disco team medals.

Disco eventually evolved into Freestyle, which now has its own branch. Breakdancing also evolved into Street Dance. Whilst most of this was happening in the dance world, I had a private life which, too, changed dramatically in the 1980s.

> ## DO YOU KNOW HOW TO DANCE THE NEW YORK BUS STOP?
> I have written out the steps in Appendix II.

Meanwhile, back in the real world, I learnt to drive and bought my first car. My mother was diagnosed with early onset senility (dementia) and my father became her full-time carer. I returned to college, obtained my B. Ed and returned to part-time teaching in school. Then, in 1985, my marriage broke down, I got divorced, my mother died, and my father remarried. I would love to say dancing helped me to sail through all of that, but I would be lying. It did, however, help tremendously. These were my darkest times, and I didn't know how to cope; but, in that year, I also met 'the one'.

When ringing (church) bells, I heard dance music and enquired. It was the best thing I've ever done. Dancing, or

rather learning to dance, is a most rewarding experience.
It has given me so much back, helped my brain to keep alert
and I am fitter than friends half my age. I hope to keep up
some form of dancing as it's good for my health and well-
being.

'Dancing Queen', aged eighty-one, Eastbourne

After my husband passed away eight years ago, I went
on a cruise. They had people to dance with, singles in the
ballroom, I thought it was such fun.
I now do group sequence dancing, group ballroom and
Latin, and I have a weekly private lesson. Four years ago, I
met another man. We have been together since and now we
dance together. If I can sum up for you what dance means
to me, it's fun, energising and good for my body.

Jools, Bournemouth

CHAPTER 8

New Beginnings

One Friday night, I went to a pub which had a rock and roll band playing. The friends I usually met were not there that night, so I stood at the bar, listening to the music as I drank my lager and black. I planned to return home when I had finished my drink.

Then, a man, also standing at the bar, introduced himself and said, "The lady I usually dance with is not here this evening. Do you jive?"

I replied, "A little."

"Would you like to dance then?" he said, preparing to step onto the dance floor.

That was almost forty years ago. We are married and still dance together. His name is Chris, and he is eleven years older than me. He saw the film *Rock Around the Clock* when it was first released. He, and his girlfriend at the time, decided to learn this new dance and became very good at it. I, on the other hand, had been dancing ballroom Jive all my life, although I had a little experience of Rock and Roll.

It did not matter that we had different styles though. He has an amazing sense of rhythm and is a very good leader, so it did not take long for us to become a couple in dancing and in life. We would go to a local Rock and Roll evening once or twice a week. We had a lot in common apart from dancing and would meet most evenings, except when I was at the dancing school.

Chris had never had any desire to learn ballroom dancing, but after a while, he joined a new beginners' class. He picked up the basics really quickly and made excellent progress. The experience and skills he learnt in his class were of immense help once I set up on my own.

I had just returned to full-time teaching when I met Chris. After a few years, I wanted to take on more responsibility at work and I secured a post as head of learning support. However, this involved moving to another part of the country. Chris said he wanted to be with me, and we moved to our first home.

The move meant leaving the dancing school too. It was hard saying goodbye to all the friends I had made there, and I still treasure their leaving presents.

I was excited about my new life and for the first few months, my feet hardly touched the floor. Then, as life settled down, I got withdrawal symptoms from dancing. The first one was that I had no children's classes to go to on Saturday mornings. Also, although we went out to local pubs, they were not licenced for dancing. There was only one ballroom school in the area, and they did not need any more teachers, so I decided to start my own school.

I saw an advert in a dance magazine from someone who had retired and was selling his variable speed record player and speakers. I thought about buying it for a while because of the cost but decided it would pay for itself once the school was up and running.

There was a pub near us with a lovely ballroom floor in its function room. They offered it to us at a good rate for one evening a week and Saturday mornings. We advertised the classes but had no idea whether anyone would turn up. I was really nervous that first night. Would anyone come? Would they like our teaching methods? Would they like us? Would they come back?

I need not have worried. They did all four. I ran the classes along the same lines as George and people began to make progress. We ran more classes. Then I got a phone call from the local further education college. It was a lovely lady called Jane, who ran the adult education classes. The couple who ran the ballroom classes were retiring and did Chris and I want to take them over? We accepted and developed a close working relationship with the college. The principal of the college and his wife actually joined one of our classes and took medal examinations.

Around that time, a new dance craze hit the country: Country and Western Line Dancing. I went to lectures; bought the music, the boots, the hats; and we started teaching that style too. Chris and I both had full-time jobs, so life was getting busy.

Chris, unfortunately, had a heart attack and had to cut down his dancing, but he was always there for big classes and special events such as medal presentations and our Christmas parties. He is a real people person, so he was great on the mike and at encouraging people to dance.

Meanwhile, I moved from working in schools and became employed by the local authority as a behaviour specialist. Eventually, I had the opportunity to take early retirement. This enabled me to return to teaching part-time but gave me more time to add more dance classes. I ran after-school clubs, took hen party sessions, taught wedding first dance choreography and cheerleading. I also added Rock and Roll, Salsa, and Latin American Line Dancing to my college repertoire. I loved this, as every day was different.

When *Strictly* came onto our TV screens and introduced the American Smooth and the Charleston, I taught these styles too, but all the time I kept up my teaching of ballroom Latin and sequence. One examiner once said to me she enjoyed my exam sessions, as they had such variety.

When I reached sixty-five, I started to cut back a bit. My body was beginning to complain, and I wanted to spend more time with my husband. However, we had been running bi-annual tea dances for the church we attend, and in 2019, we started planning a special tea dance for the local community to celebrate the seventy-fifth anniversary of the end of World War II. By February 2020, the plans were complete, and I had started teaching my pupils dances like the Palais Glide and Under the Spreading Chestnut Tree. Then, in March, along came Covid and the first long lockdown, so that never happened.

When things started to open up again, the necessary social distancing controls made it hard for dancing teachers. People could only dance together if they were in the same bubble and most of my pupils came without a partner. We had to make sure that people did not get too close to each other, and we got used to dancing wearing hats, scarves and gloves due to having doors and windows open.

Dance teachers went shopping. We bought visors, plastic gloves, detergent, anti-bacterial spray, hand gel and masking tape. Why the masking tape, I hear you ask? Well, we had to mark the floor out in rectangles or squares big enough to keep people safe. We were given a mathematical formula to work this out. I used the squares like a chess board using only the white squares. The masking tape was used to mark out these squares. This reduced the number of people in the classes and many people who stopped dancing for lockdown never returned.

These restrictions worked okay for my Line Dancing groups but I had to ensure that people kept to the social dancing regulations before and after class, so the social interaction, which gives life to a class, could not happen. My pupils still enjoyed attending though, which helped them cope with that difficult period.

Ballroom classes were more problematic. The standard dances of Waltz, Quickstep, Foxtrot and Tango have been developed for over one hundred years to travel around the room, but that could not happen because I could not ensure that people remained socially distanced. I developed special little ballroom routines which would keep the individual or couple within their space by changing amounts of turn and changing the order of figures. Ballroom is designed as a couple activity, and they work together. However, many of my pupils were singletons and found it difficult to dance solo. They said they would prefer to wait until all restrictions were lifted, so our ballroom class stopped again for several months.

Things were different after Covid. Many people no longer felt strong enough or brave enough to return to social settings and some could no longer afford it. Also, the reason many people came to ballroom classes changed. In my area, we had lots of charity balls and many large hotels hosting wedding receptions. Many of my pupils initially came to enjoy themselves at such events but those events no longer happen.

I decided to ask my pupils post-Covid why they were attending. There were three reasons:

- to mix with other people
- to learn a new skill
- to do something with their partner.

Learning this enabled me to adjust the style and content of my classes.

It came as a shock to everyone, my husband included, when I announced, in 2023, my intention to close the dancing school and retire, and it happened quickly. I decided in February, announced it in March and organised a last dance for April. It was not a retirement dance but rather a celebration. I had realised that it was sixty years since my first ballroom class, so I advertised it as 'A Celebration of 60 Years as a Ballroom Dancer'. We all thoroughly enjoyed ourselves. I organised banners, balloons and a cake. I received cards, presents and flowers, for which I am very grateful, but what I enjoyed the most was seeing so many of my pupils, both past and present, dancing and having fun. That was my reward. That is the reward of all dance teachers. It is not just about teaching people to dance. It is about seeing them enjoying themselves. It is about the positive changes dancing brings to people's lives. It is about delivering happiness.

Both Sue and I are 'second time arounders', i.e. we have been married before. When we got together (thirty-five years ago), we decided that we needed some exercise and to pursue an activity that neither of us had done before. We decided on dancing... Dancing is one of the only ways I can hold the wife and prance around in public without too much comment from bystanders. We still thoroughly enjoy dancing and will continue for as long as we are able.

Pete, Bournemouth

CHAPTER 9

Why Dance?

My immediate response to that question is: why not? Dancing has been proved scientifically to improve physical, emotional and mental health. It widens your social circle. It opens up avenues to continually learn new skills and develop creativity, in addition to enhancing memory skills. It is accessible to people of all ages and you may, like me, find a life partner.

Let us look at the physical health first.

> 'Taken seriously it (ballroom dancing) gives the young person as much physical exercise as is desired; to the middle-aged dancer, it can give you exercise that is effective without being too strenuous; to the busy man or woman it will provide that mental relaxation which is necessary to physical health.'
> *Ballroom Dancing* by Alex Moore, page 2 of the 1945 edition.

We have over six hundred muscles in our body, and they are all controlled by our brain. It is not only our feet and legs we use when we dance, but our arms for balance and hold, our torso for posture and poise, and our head for balance and effect. Dancing raises our heart rate and gets the blood pumping around the body. It also improves our lung function. Dancing regularly will improve the way you walk, your balance and your stance, which are all of particular importance as you age. *The British Medical Journal* of September 2019 even reported that dancing results in lower rates of cancers and cardiovascular disease.

This physical activity also impacts positively on your mental health. It is because exercise boosts mood and a general sense of well-being that some doctors are prescribing dance and exercise classes instead of anti-depressants to some patients. The exercise results in the release of endorphins. These are brain chemicals which give you the 'feel-good factor'. Doing such exercise regularly maximises these effects and if you are part of a class, you are likely to keep up the exercise because you are also enjoying social interaction and the mutual support of your classmates.

When you are learning, and practising, a new physical skill such as dancing, you have to concentrate on what you are doing. You are therefore mindful of what you are doing and that can block out worries and negative thoughts. In my darkest days, when I did not want to get out of bed, let alone dance, I always knew that dancing would improve my mood, so I would get myself ready and stand in front of a mirror. Then I would sing a chorus of the song 'Smile' to my reflection. I could then make it to the studio. Once I started dancing, or teaching it, I would focus completely on that. Indeed, the act of dancing can sometimes just make us happy. Only yesterday, I attended a ballet class which really stretched me physically and mentally. I cannot say that I performed wonderfully, but when we had danced our little routine to the music, I felt truly happy and full of joy. It released the inner child within me, and I felt great.

The class I attend is for more mature learners; the eldest is well into her nineties. We come from all walks of life and range widely in shape, age and height, but that does not matter; we are a class. We worry when someone is missing. We care for people when they are in distress; we celebrate with them; we welcome new members; and we care for each other. I attend a Tap dancing class which is exactly the same. The care is evidenced by the chat in our WhatsApp group chats.

In the frontispiece of *Ballroom Dancing for Beginners and Bronze Medallists*, first edition by the IDMA (1950), it states, 'what you learn will give you endless pleasure in years to come for dancing is a social pastime and through it you will make new friends'.

I have mentioned feeling happy when I dance; some dancers have been known to cry at the end of a performance. This is partly due to our emotional response to music. For me, dancing the Rumba is always an emotional journey and I enjoy dancing it solo in an empty room which enables me to move freely and wherever the inner me takes me.

When you dance, you also affect those watching. Think about the impact that a war dance has on the opposing side, or a rugby team before a match. I once went to an amazing performance of the ballet *Carmen* when I actually felt I had been moved momentarily to a higher plane. I was glad that I had attended alone, as what I experienced was beyond words.

And the bit about meeting a new life partner? Well, that happens a lot. I am a case in point, but why? Obviously, you both have at least one interest in common, but if you dance regularly with someone, you also talk to each other and get to know one another. You also learn to trust each other. When Chris first led me into a double spin where he released hold of me, I had to be sure that he would be there at the end to collect me or catch me if I lost balance. There is also the theory that women are attracted to good male dancers, as they see them as good physical mating material. I could not possibly comment on that.

Throughout this book, you will have seen, and I hope read, small textboxes containing *quotes*. These are from ordinary people expressing what dance means to them. Why don't you give it a try and see how it affects you? I have included a list of organisations you can contact to find out what dance opportunities there are in your area, but it is not finite. You can also talk to friends and look at Facebook, for example. Somewhere, there is a dance class perfect for you, so why not dance?

Dance is the activity that has it all: fun, friendship and fitness. Learning a new dance is a great challenge, both for your body and your mind. And where you have dance, you also have music, music, music.
What's not to like?

Paul, Eastbourne

This next quote comes from my ballet and tap teacher, who has become a great friend along the way.

Well, I was born pigeon-toed and at the age of five, went to the doctor's. His answer... 'Take her to ballet, that will help.' Well, fifty-two years later and I'm still dancing, still teaching, still choreographing and still running my original dance school. Of course, I have cut down a little, and need holiday rests, but dance has kept me going through all the good and bad time. It raises your spirit and releases joy. So, if you haven't started, then begin... if you are dancing, carry on till you dance in heaven. I shall definitely be dancing up the path to the pearly gates.

Glynis, Principal Willingdon School of Dancing

Epilogue: What Next?

I have not stopped dancing. Like Glynis, I will be dancing along the path to the pearly gates.

I now attend a Folk Dancing class, a dance fitness group, a ballet class, a Tap class and a ballroom class attended by some of my ex-pupils and run by a colleague. I performed on stage in Glynis's latest Christmas production.

Are there any other styles of dance I could try? Maybe, but I have already ticked off Jazz and Belly Dancing. I may enter inventive dance competitions, as I love choreography. Maybe I will invent a dance that people will still be dancing in twenty, or fifty years' time. Who knows? I may write more books about dancing. I am taking a course in podcasting, so that will be a new avenue to explore. Maybe I will become a motivational speaker, but one thing is for sure: I WILL STILL BE DANCING.

And if I am allowed to quote myself?

'When I am alone with music playing, and with at least 2m^2 of floor area, I will dance. When I dance, I become part of the music and my inner self takes control of my body in order to express my feelings and expel stress, leaving me calm and happy when the endorphins take over.'

Yvonne Wright, 2024

Appendix I

Dance Information

Chapter 1

The Twist
According to Nornie Dwyer in her book *Dance the Twist*, '...the dance became popular when a newspaper columnist dropped into a New York teenage haunt called the Peppermint Lounge. .. with the next day's paper, the twist was on its way... To Paris, Rome – right through the continent to Britain.' Page 2.

For a while, the country went Twist crazy. Lots of artists and pop groups were releasing Twist music and I still think 'Twist and Shout' was one of The Beatles' best records. When everyone started dancing the Twist, the shops were filled with Twist dresses.

To dance the Twist, stand with the feet slightly apart with the weight over the balls of the feet. Now, just swivel the feet and hips using your arms to enhance the swivel. You can dance it solo, with a partner or in a group.

There are a wide range of variations on the basic Twist. These include:

- Twisting down to the floor then popping up like a cork released from a bottle – you can incorporate a half turn to end back-to-back with a partner, or a full turn, or one person does a full turn the other half to end one person behind the other.
- Leaning forward and back, or side to side, as you twist.
- Moving around your partner, or group members, as you twist.
- Any other move you want.

The Hokey Cokey
This originated from an English Folk dance as early as 1826. It was very popular as a party dance in the 1940s. It has been danced around the world but with different names.

The Quickstep
The Quickstep has its origins in the Charleston dance craze of the 1920s. In England, dancers started taking out the kicks and merging it with the Foxtrot. It was originally known as the Fast Foxtrot and also incorporated the One-Step, the March, the Peabody and the Black Bottom. It was first standardised in 1927.

Chapter 2

The Circle Waltz
This is a group dance in Waltz time. It is danced in a circle. It is progressive, this means you change partners, and it is based on a folk dance.

The Waltz
The word 'Waltz' means to roll or revolve. It is danced in triple time, i.e. one, two, three. It developed from a thirteenth-century folk dance in the areas now known as Germany and Austria. The

modern Waltz evolved from a folk dance during the eighteenth century into what we know today as the Viennese Waltz. When it was introduced to England, it was known as 'the forbidden dance' due to way the gentleman held his partner closely to him. He also placed his hand on his partner's back, which led to all men wearing white gloves when dancing; this is still a requirement of classical sequence. The dance only became respectable when royalty started dancing it; the Emperor of Russia and Queen Victoria were fans of this new dance.

The 'slow' or 'English' Waltz, as it sometimes known, evolved from the Viennese Waltz during the twentieth century. There are other variations too, including:

- The Boston Waltz; slower than the Viennese, with fewer turns.
- The American Waltz; danced to a slower Viennese rhythm of quick quick slow but has four quarter turns rather than the two half turns of the Viennese version.

Cha Cha Cha

This dance has its origins in Cuba and was developed as a ballroom dance in the 1950s. It, and its first cousins the Rumba and Mambo, is danced on the second beat in the bar. It also has a syncopation, where two or more steps are danced on one beat of music, so its count is two, three, four and one. This timing is very difficult for beginners to understand at first.

Rumba

According to the *History of English Ballroom Dancing* by Phillip Richardson, the Rumba rhythm was first heard in New York in 1931, and the leading person in England to develop this dance was Monsieur Pierre. It is my favourite Latin American dance, as I am able to express my emotions through my body and my arms.

The Foxtrot
Harry Fox created this dance in 1914. It was initially very jerky, not like the flowing dance we have today. It was 'tamed' by dance teachers over time with the hops and kicks being removed. These were later reintroduced to the Fast Foxtrot, i.e. the Quickstep.

The Tango
The Tango is an amalgamation of dances. It has its origins in nineteenth-century Haiti and Cuba; it then travelled to Argentina and was danced in the poorer areas of Buenos Aires. Europeans travelling to Argentina brought the dance back to Paris and the Tango arrived in Britain in 1912. It was considered quite daring but became extremely popular and Tango teas became very common. The Ballroom Tango bears little resemblance to the original, but the Argentine Tango is now popular once more.

> *I love the way the music and the dancing makes me feel happy.*
>
> Helen T, Eastbourne

Chapter 3

The Veleta
This dance was created by Arthur Morris in 1900 and is danced in Waltz time. It was reputedly, the first sequence dance. Before then, there were set dances such as the Lancers. In 1950, Victor Sylvester estimated that there were six hundred sequence dances. Currently, the number stands at over five thousand, though many of them are no longer danced.

The Boston Two Step
This is one of the best known Two Steps. The Two Step itself evolved from the Washington Post March and is danced in six/eight time.

The Boston Two Step was created in 1908 by Tom Walton. It is known for its use of a step called a pas de basque, which did indeed originate in the Basque region of France and is similar to the balance step in ballet. Most of my pupils know it as the hello goodbye step, as I taught them that as they danced a pas de basque away from their partner, they should turn their head towards their partner as if saying hello. When they danced one towards their partner, they should turn their head away from their partner as if saying goodbye.

Another famous Two Step is the Military Two Step. This was arranged by James Finnigan in 1906. It involves the gentleman saluting his partner, whilst his partner bobs a curtsey. It is not often danced these days, as half the dance is waltzing, and many people feel it is too tiring.

Saunter Reve
The Saunter is a slow dance similar, in some ways, to the Ballroom Foxtrot. It has a leisurely, graceful walking movement. The feet are closed in parallel position rather than the turned-out position of ballet used for Two Steps and Old-Time Waltz. One of the earliest saunters was the Moonlight, composed in 1919 by Charles Daniels. However, the Saunter Reve was relatively modern when I learnt it, as it was created by Rita Pover in 1961.

Old Time (Classical) Tango
This is similar to the Ballroom Tango, but the poise and hold are different. This means that the basic walk differs between the two styles. The Tango Serida is still extremely popular. Towards the end, the lady makes a full solo turn away from her partner, who then brings her back towards him. I notice nowadays that many older ladies just walk away rather than turn. However, I still love to dance the turn, and I will continue to do it for as long as I am able. It was also created by Ria Pover in 1961.

Chapter 4

Samba
Ballroom Samba is a lively, rhythmical dance which has evolved from the Brazilian Samba. It is complicated because it has several different actions and timings. The one taught first, to most people learning the dance, is the bounce action with a timing of one and a two and a one and two. There are many different holds, and unlike Rumba, Samba, and Jive, which are fairly stationary, it travels around the room.

Jive
Ballroom Jive has evolved from elements of the Jitterbug, Lindy Hop, Swing, and Rock and Roll. I always explain to my pupils that they should think of Jive as a tree. I teach them what I call 'Social Jive', which has a timing of slow, slow, quick, quick and explain that this is the trunk of the tree. There are several branches on the tree which include:

- The more formal Ballroom Jive, which has a chasse base with a timing of Q a Q Q a Q QQ.
- Le roc or Ceroc, which evolved in France when disco was evolving in the late '60s and the '70s in Britain, and was danced to jazz music, which was popular in France at the time.
- Rock and roll, which is much more relaxed and became popular following the release of the film *Rock Around the Clock* in 1956. It has a simple basic step but can be acrobatic and is danced to a wide variety of tempi.

Chapter 5

Technique
When you first learn ballroom dancing, you need to know:

- Where to place your feet; in the technique book, that comes under the heading of 'Positions of Feet'.
- When to move your feet, which comes under 'Timing'.
- Which part, or parts, of the foot to use; that comes under 'Footwork'.
- As you become more accomplished, you learn other aspects of technique such as Rise and Fall and Sway.
- This technique has been developed over the last one hundred years and continues to evolve because dance is an art form and therefore has no finite borders. The technique, taught to you by a good teacher, enables you to develop as a dancer and be the best you can be.

Chapter 6

When we had a party night, there was a range of novelty dances that everyone enjoyed. Here are a few.

The Palais Glide
This is a party dance dating from the mid 1930s. Lines of up to six people stand next to each other with their arms around each other. The steps are easy to pick up and we always played it on New Year's Eve.

The Lambeth Walk
This also dates from the mid 1930s but is danced with a partner. It is danced to the title song of the musical *The Lambeth Walk*. It is memorable for everyone, joining in with "Oi!" and pushing their thumb over their shoulder at the same time.

Hands Knees and Bumps a Daisy
This dance was featured in the musical *Bandwagon* starring Arthur Askey. The song tells you what to do; tap your hands

to your partner's hand, tap your hands to your own knees then turn away from your partner and hit your hip to your partner's hip. As the song progresses, you do double and treble hits, which can be great fun.

The Conga

The Conga originates from a Cuban carnival dance of the same name. Everyone stands in a line, one behind the other, holding onto the waist of the person in front. The steps are quite easy; three forward steps and a small kick to the side, which is repeated continuously. The person at the front is the leader and wherever she/he goes, everyone must follow without breaking the chain. It is common for them to lead you round in ever decreasing circles and then out again.

Dance has benefited both my physical and mental health. It makes me so happy to be moving with the rhythm of the music. There are always new steps and routines to learn so it has become a never-ending journey of joy and discovery for me.

Sue M, Eastbourne

Chapter 7

New York Bus Stop

I have been told this dance was created at a bus stop in New York but that is probably an urban myth. To dance it, you start with your feet together.

1   Step sideways with your right foot.
2   Close your left foot to your right foot.
3   Step sideways with your right foot.

4   Tap your left foot to your right foot.

5–8 Now go side together, side tap to the left.

9   Point your right foot forwards and across your left foot.

10   Point your right foot back and sideways.

11   Using your right foot, step forward and across your left foot.

12   Point your left foot to the side.

13   Step forwards and across your right foot with your left foot.

14   Point your right foot to the side.

15   Step forwards and across your left foot with your right foot.

16   Keeping your feet where they are, just transfer your weight backwards onto your left foot.

Now repeat. If you turn your body to the right as you step across with your right foot, you can make the dance turn in a clockwise direction.

Chapter 8

Charleston

This dance is associated with the flappers of the 1920s. The World War I had ended with a terrible loss of life and the young people wanted to enjoy life to the full. Women's hemlines rose. Jazz, Tango and Ragtime music became popular, and their dancing became wild and, to many, outrageous. Dances like the Black Bottom, the Breakaway and the Charleston fitted the bill.

The Charleston is named after Charleston in South Carolina, where the dance was discovered and brought to England. Initially, it was danced on stage, but in July 1925, a magazine called *The Dancing Times* arranged a tea dance for people to learn the Charleston. From there, it became immensely popular.

Who to Contact

International Dance Teachers Association www.idta.co.uk
Imperial Society of Teachers of Dancing www.istd.org.uk
National Association of Teachers of Dancing www.natd.org.uk
One Dance UK www.onedanceuk.org.uk
British Theatre Dance Association www.btda.org.uk
UKA Dance www.ukadance.co.uk
British Association of Teachers of Dancing www.batd.co.uk
The U3a (University of the Third Age)
Your local authority
Your local further education college
Community centres
Search for a dance school/class near you

Bibliography

Dance and Rhythm Periodical Vol 1 No 3, Jan 1949

Dance the Twist, Nornie Dwyer, Brittania, 1960s (exact year unknown)

Discotheque Dancing, Doris Lavelle, Self, 1970

Latin and American Dancing, M. Pierre Thomason 1948

Let's Dance: Social, Ballroom, & Folk Dancing, Peter Buckman, Paddington, 1978

The Dance Cure, Dr Peter Lovatt, Short Books, 2020

The Girls' Book of Ballroom Dancing, Vera Wilson Burke, 1959

The History of Ballroom Dancing, Philip JS Richardson, Herbert Jenkins, 1940

The Official Guide to Disco Dance Steps, Jack and K Vallari, Hamlyn, 1979

The Story of British Popular Dance, Lyndon Wainwright, ID Publications, 1996

Three Hundred Hints on Modern Dancing, Edward Scott, Allen & Unwin, 1923

Milton Keynes UK
Ingram Content Group UK Ltd.
UKHW050627311024
2488UKWH00056B/419